CONQUERING SURVIVOR

Something Powerful

by

Deborah Ann Tome
(M.S.S.W., L.C.S.W.)

Disclaimer: The information contained in this book is based on the professional experience and personal journey of the author. It is intended for motivational and educational purposes only and does not constitute medical or psychological advice. The reader should consult with a healthcare professional before making any health-related decisions.

First Edition: April 2026

DEDICATION

To my daughter, Danielle. You are the heartbeat behind my resilience. You are the future I fight for. May you never face the burdens I carried, but if you do, may you find the strength within yourself to conquer them. You are my Why.

To my dad, Johnny. You were my steadfast support when I was small. In a world that often felt uncertain, you were the solid ground beneath my feet. Thank you for showing me what safety feels like, and for being the foundation that allowed me to stand tall.

To my brother, Patrick. You were a true genius who made me humble. Your abstract thinking was extraordinary, and your landscapes showed me beauty where others saw only canvas. Caring for you during your final days was difficult, but I wouldn't trade those moments for anything. They were sacred. You taught me that love is stronger than death. You are missed, but never forgotten.

This book is for you.

CONTENTS

INTRODUCTION
The Warrior's Call

There is a phrase that sits on the cover of this book, two words that terrify the human mind more than almost any others: "Don't Know."

We are wired to crave certainty. When trauma hits, whether it is the sharp shock of a sudden loss, the dull ache of a toxic childhood, or a medical crisis that leaves you gasping for air, our brains scramble for answers. Why did this happen? Who am I now? Am I safe?

When the answer is "I don't know," we often freeze. We feel like a ship without a rudder, drifting in a dark ocean. We start to view ourselves as broken, as victims, as "sick."

I am writing this book to challenge that narrative.

I have sat across from hundreds of patients who come to me with a "sack of stones" on their backs, heavy burdens of guilt, resentment, and trauma.

They look at me and say, "I don't know who I am anymore." I tell them: That is exactly where you need to be.

"Don't Know" is not a void. It is the birthplace of the Warrior. If you don't know who you were, you are free to decide who you will be.

My purpose in these pages is not just to help you survive. Survival is the baseline. Survival is getting out of bed when you want to hide. But there is a progression to the human spirit that most people never complete. We start as Victims—things happen to us. With work, we become Survivors—we made it through. But the goal of this book is to get you to the third stage: the **Warrior**.

The Warrior doesn't just survive the fire; they look back at the fire and say, "I am happy I endured that."

That sounds radical, doesn't it? To be happy, you endured pain? But through my own battles, facing death at 19, surviving strokes, and navigating the terror of a stalker, I learned that we don't have to carry the damage as a sickness. We can wear it as armor.

"It's not possible to recover from your own soul's death without regurgitating the bitterness of what has been."

— **Lisa A. Romano**

This book is a guide to weaving your trauma into resilience. It is about refusing to view events as losses and seeing them only as lessons.

Welcome to the Shift.

CHAPTER 1
The Core Philosophy: Conquering Survivor's

I was nineteen years old when the lights almost went out.

At nineteen, you are supposed to be immortal. You are supposed to be thinking about your next date, your college classes, or the weekend. You are not supposed to be lying in a hospital bed, hovering on the thin, terrifying line between being here and being... nowhere.

I almost died that year. It wasn't a gentle fading; it was a violent interruption of the script I thought my life was following.

When you come that close to the edge, everything non-essential gets stripped away. The petty arguments, the social anxieties, the plans for five years down the road, they all evaporate. You are left with a stark, brutal clarity. In that darkness, fear is the loudest thing in the room. But right underneath the fear, if you listen closely, there is something else.

There is a lesson.

I survived. I came back from the edge. But the physical recovery was only half the battle. The real war was in my mind. I had to decide how to categorize what had just happened to me. The world wanted to give me a label. They wanted to call me a "victim" of illness. They wanted me to be fragile. They wanted me to ask, "Why did this happen to me?"

If I had asked "Why," I would have stayed stuck in that hospital bed forever, even after I was discharged. "Why" is a victim's question. It looks backward. It looks for blame.

Instead, I found the phrase that would become the heartbeat of my entire life and career: **Conquering Survivor's**

I decided that I didn't suffer a loss of health; I gained a terrifying appreciation for life. I didn't lose my sense of safety; I gained the knowledge that I am resilient enough to survive the worst.

In those moments, I felt a presence—something greater than myself—

guiding me, reminding me that even in the darkest times, there's a force at work, helping me rise. This was not just a physical recovery… it was a spiritual awakening, a lesson in resilience.

Through every trauma, and there have been many, from strokes to death scares, I learned that you have to suffer loss to have gain.

The Cyberstalker and the Shift

Years later, I faced a different kind of darkness—cyberstalking.

It's a unique kind of terror, where you feel hunted, and your sense of autonomy is violated. Your own space, your home, can begin to feel like a cage. The instinct is to shrink, to hide, and to make yourself as small as possible so the threat passes over.

For a long time, I struggled with the trauma of it. I felt the walls closing in. But then, the "Warrior" mindset kicked in. I refused to just be a victim of stalking; I had to find the gain.

I looked at that terror and asked, "What is this pushing me to do?"

It became clear to me that my purpose was expanding. The experience forced me out of my comfort zone, making me realize that I needed to reach more people, not fewer. It pushed me to explore new opportunities, to speak to larger audiences, and to share my message with as many people as I could.

The intent to silence me became a lesson: to detach, I needed to be louder. I felt God's presence guiding me through the ordeal. His help gave me the strength to rise above the fear and use it as a tool for empowerment.

That is the difference between a Victim and a Warrior. A Victim hides from the trauma. A Warrior uses the trauma as fuel. The money, the fame, the TV shows, those weren't the purpose. The purpose was that the trauma clarified my mission: I needed to reach people and tell them they can survive, too.

The "Sickness" Trap

This brings me to why I am writing this book, and why I approach therapy differently than many of my peers.

We have a habit in the mental health field and in society at large of treating trauma survivors as if they are permanently "sick." We look at their wounds and say, "Oh, you poor thing. You are broken."

I hate that.

I tell my patients, and I am telling you now, I want you to come from a perspective of being happy that you endured these things.

That sounds insane to the average person. Happy that I was stalked?

Happy that I had a stroke?

Yes. Because if you survived it, you have data that other people don't have. You have proof of your own strength. You have navigated hell and walked out the other side. That isn't a sickness; that is a superpower.

When patients come to me, they often say, "I don't know who I am." They have been people-pleasing, enabling, and hiding for so long that they have lost their identity. They feel like a collection of symptoms.

My job isn't to hold their hand and agree that they are sick. My job is to help them find out who they really are underneath the trauma. We strip away the "victim" label. We look at the "losses": the bad childhood, the abusive ex, the scary diagnosis, and we mine them for gold.

The Physics of Growth

Here is the hard truth: **You cannot grow in comfort.**
Comfort is stagnation. Growth happens in the friction. It happens in the "loss."

- You lose a relationship. You learn the lesson of your own boundaries.
- You lose a job. You learn the lesson of your own resourcefulness.
- You lose your health. You learn the lesson of what truly matters.

I have learned that I can be totally flat broke, facing financial ruin, and I don't collapse. I go, "Okay. Got to make some money." That isn't denial. That is the ultimate confidence that comes from knowing you have survived 100% of your bad days.

This book is not about erasing your past. It is not about pretending the bad things didn't hurt. It is about refusing to let those bad things own you.

We are going to reframe your history. We are going to stop counting the scars and start counting the lessons. You are not a victim. You are not even just a survivor.

You are a Warrior in training. And Warriors don't tally their losses. They only tally what they've learned.

Actionable Step: The Reframing Protocol

I want you to start this practice immediately. We are going to take the "loss" that is currently weighing heaviest on your mind and flip it.

The Exercise:

1. **Identify the "Loss":** Write down the one event or circumstance that makes you feel most like a victim right now. (e.g., "My partner left me," "I was fired," "I had a scary medical diagnosis").

2. **The Victim Script:** Write down what your fear is telling you about this. (e.g., "I am unlovable," "I am a failure," "I am weak").

3. **The Warrior Script:** Now, I want you to force your brain to find the lesson. It doesn't have to be pretty. It just has to be a gain.

   - *Instead of "I am alone," write:* "I have learned that I can stand on my own two feet without needing someone to prop me up."

   - *Instead of "I am broke," write:* "I am learning exactly how resourceful I can be when my back is against the wall."

Do not leave this chapter until you have found one lesson. That is your spark. That is where we begin.

CHAPTER 2
The Fuel of Determination and Purpose

There is a statistic I share with my clients that usually wakes them up.

If you come to therapy and you just sit in the chair for an hour a week, you have about a **30% chance** of getting better. But, if you come to therapy, take notes, and actually *do the homework* I give you outside of this office? Your success rate shoots up to **90%**.

I can give you every tool in the world. I can explain your trauma, your attachment style, and your triggers. But I cannot give you the will to use them. We are a team. My part is giving you the skills; your part is getting it done.

That "getting it done" factor? That is **Determination**. And in my experience, determination isn't something you are born with. It is often something that is forged in the fire of devastation.

The $400 Lesson

I want to tell you where my determination came from. It wasn't a happy moment. It was one of the loneliest moments of my life.

I was in my early twenties. My father had just died. I had spent the previous year taking care of him; he was demanding, often calling the police or the church, thinking people were stealing from him, and I was the only one there. Because I was his full-time caregiver, I wasn't working. I had no money.

I have a genetic blood-clotting disorder. If I don't take my medication, I have strokes. I had already faced death at 19. Now, with my father gone, I needed $400 to buy the medicine that kept me alive.

$400. That was the price of my survival.
I went to my family. These were the people who were supposed to be my safety net. I asked them for the money. They all said no.

They didn't care if I lived or died. That is what that refusal said to me. It wasn't just about the money; it was the realization that **I was completely alone**.

I had two choices in that moment.

1. **Collapse:** I could have curled up, sunk into depression, and accepted that I was unloved and helpless.

2. **Conquer:** I could decide that if I was going to survive, *I* had to be the one to ensure it.

That devastation triggered my determination. It was a turning point. I realized, "If things are going to be done, I am going to do them." I started working part-time, then full-time, despite my health. I pulled myself up not because I wanted to, but because I *had* to.

Determination is the prerequisite for recovery. You have to look at your trauma and say, "I am determined to make something of myself, regardless of who is or isn't standing beside me."

The Purpose Vacuum

Once you have the determination to move, you need a direction to move *in.* This is where **Purpose** comes in.
I see so many clients who are drifting. They are going through the motions of life, waking up, working, sleeping, but they have no "North Star." When you have no purpose, you are vulnerable. When a crisis hits, you don't have a reason to push through it. You feel like a victim because you don't know where you are going.

Purpose is the path. It guides you through the hills and valleys. If you have a purpose, you can endure the "valleys" (the suffering) because you know you are hiking toward a specific peak.

"Life is never made unbearable by circumstances, only by lack of meaning and purpose."

— **Victor Frankl**

The Evolution of Purpose

One of the biggest mistakes people make is thinking they need to find one giant "Life Purpose" that lasts forever. The truth is, purpose evolves. It shifts as we age. In my practice, I see this progression clearly:

The 20s: The Search for Identity – At 25, most people don't know who they are. They are just trying to separate from their families. Their "purpose" is often just *getting away* or having fun. They don't have a solid identity yet. It's mostly **Exploration.**

- *The Warrior's Shift:* If you are in this stage, your purpose is simply

Exploration. You are gathering data on what you like and what you hate.

The 30s: Solidifying the Path – By 35, you usually know what you want. You've been working for ten or fifteen years. You know if you hate your job. You know if you want a family. This is where purpose becomes about **Building**.

The Motherhood Factor – For many women, purpose becomes instinctual when they have children. Biology kicks in. Your purpose is *them.* For men, it's often different. They don't always have that immediate nurturing instinct, but they find purpose in *providing* for the family. This is a valid, powerful season of purpose.

The 40s: The Midlife Pivot – At 45, things get tricky. You realize you aren't young anymore. You start seeing the end of the road. Some people panic ("midlife crisis") because they realize they haven't lived the life they wanted.

- *The Warrior's Shift:* This is the time to **Re-evaluate**. It is not too late to pivot.

The Retirement Trap (60s+) – I see a lot of depression in retired people. They spent 40 years with a purpose (work), and suddenly, it's gone. They have empty days. They wither because they have no "Why."

The Warrior's Shift: You must find a new mission. It doesn't have to be a job. It can be volunteering, mentoring, or creating. You cannot live without a target.

Visualization: The Ecology of You

How do you find your purpose if you feel lost? **Visualization.**
I had a client recently, a young man in his late 20s. He felt stuck. I asked him, "What do you want to do?" He said, "I love ecology. I want to save the planet." I asked him to close his eyes. "Picture yourself in five years. Where are you?"

He closed his eyes and smiled. "I'm in Washington, D.C. I'm an activist. I'm speaking on a stage about the environment." "That," I told him, "Is your purpose."

Once he saw that image, the Activist in D.C., we could work backward.

- Does his current job get him there? No.
- What steps does he need to take today? Maybe volunteering on weekends. Maybe finding a job as an air pollution evaluator.

  When he visualized the destination, the path became clear. He realized he could take a smaller job now (like an air pollution evaluator) because it was a stepping stone to the big dream. It gave him patience and drive.

Actionable Step: The Values Audit

You cannot find your purpose if you don't know your **Values**.

If you don't know what matters to you, you can't know where you should go.

- If you value **Adventure**, but you work in a cubicle, you will likely be depressed.
- If you value **Family**, but you take a job that requires 80% travel, you will be miserable.

Your Homework for Chapter 2:

1. **List Your Top 5 Values:** Is it Freedom? Security? Creativity? Helping others? Money? (Be honest if it's money, write money).
2. **The 5-Year Visualization:** Close your eyes. It is five years from

today. You are waking up.

- Where are you?
- Who is next to you?
- What are you doing for work?
- How do you *feel*?

3. **Draft a Working Purpose Statement:** Based on that visualization, write one sentence.
    - *Example:* "My purpose is to gain the skills I need to become an advocate for the environment."
    - *Example:* "My purpose right now is to provide stability for my children so they don't feel the fear I felt."

Determination is the fuel. Purpose is the map. Now, let's start driving.

CHAPTER 3
The Transformation from Victim to Survivor

There is a comfortable misery in being a victim.

I know that sounds harsh. Nobody *wants* to be traumatized. Nobody *asks* to be abused, assaulted, or abandoned. But once the event is over, the identity of the "Victim" can feel like a warm, heavy blanket. It is safe. It is passive. If you are a victim, nothing is your fault. If you are a victim, the world owes you an apology.

But here is the problem: As long as you are a victim, you are powerless.

You cannot drive the car if you are sitting in the back seat screaming about the crash.

To heal, we have to make the most critical shift in this entire process. We have to move from **Victim** (things happened to me) to **Survivor** (I navigated what happened to me).

"One may conquer millions in battle, but he who conquers himself is the greatest of conquerors."

— **Buddha**

This isn't just semantics. It is the difference between staying sick and getting well.

The Gun to My Head

I want to tell you about the moment I became a "victim" in the eyes of the law, and how I almost let it destroy me.

I was in my own driveway. I was sitting in my car, door open, one leg out on the pavement. I was listening to a song on the radio, just taking a moment before going inside.

Suddenly, a man appeared from the back of my car. The stalker put a gun a few inches away from my head.

He robbed me. He took what he wanted. And in that moment, I froze.

I didn't fight. I didn't scream. I didn't go full "action hero." I sat there, terrified, with metal pressed against my head, and I let him take it.

After he left, the police came. The report was filed. I was officially a victim of aggravated robbery. But the real damage wasn't the money he stole. The real damage was the story I started telling myself immediately after.

I blamed *myself.*

"Why was your leg out of the car, Deborah?" "Why were you just sitting there listening to music?" "You made yourself a target. You were stupid. You were weak."

For months, I couldn't go outside. I couldn't walk into my own yard. I jumped at every shadow. I was living in a cage of my own making, built out of shame and guilt. I told myself I should have fought back. I told myself I should have seen him coming.

That is the **Victim Script**. It turns the anger inward. It says, "I am damaged because I allowed this."

The shift to **Survivor** didn't happen overnight. It happened when I looked at the facts without the shame filter.

I realized: *Wait a minute. He had a gun.*

If I had fought? I'd be dead. If I had screamed? I might be dead.

I didn't freeze because I was weak. I froze because I was smart. My brain, my ancient, survival-wired brain, calculated the odds in a microsecond and said: *Stay still. Stay alive.*

That was the moment I reclaimed my power. I wasn't a pathetic woman who got robbed. I was a resilient woman who assessed a lethal threat and did exactly what was necessary to survive it 100%.

I still don't walk alone at night. That's not fear; that's wisdom. A Survivor learns from the data. But I am not afraid of my driveway anymore.

The Reptile in the Room

One of the biggest reasons people stay stuck in Victim mode is that they don't understand their own biology.

I have patients come in, heads hanging low, consumed by shame. They say, "I should have run," or "I should have fought him off," or "I don't know why I just sat there."

I tell them: **You didn't have a choice. Your reptile took over.**

When trauma hits, whether it's a car crash, an assault, or a medical crisis, your prefrontal cortex (the thinking, logical part of your brain) goes offline. It shuts down. You are now operating entirely from the amygdala and the brainstem. We call this the "Reptile Brain."

The Reptile doesn't care about your dignity. It doesn't care about your ego. It only cares about one thing: **Survival.**

Sometimes, the Reptile says *Fight.* Sometimes, it says *Flight.* But often, especially in overwhelming trauma, it chooses a third option: **Freeze.**

Clinically, we call this a *Dorsal Vagal Shutdown.* It is a biological mechanism where the body plays dead to minimize harm. It is not cowardice. It is a brilliant evolutionary adaptation.

I had a male patient once, a big guy who had been through a traumatic ordeal. He was kidnapped and taken to a warehouse, where the captors threatened his life. They told him, "If you move, we kill you. If you struggle, we kill your family." They assaulted him repeatedly, and he didn't fight back.

Years later, he came to me carrying a mountain of shame. He felt he wasn't a "man" because he didn't resist. He felt guilty for not fighting.

I told him what I'm telling you: "If you had fought, you would be dead. And your family might be dead too. Your brain made the calculation that 'Compliance = Survival.' You are not a coward. You are a hero who protected your family by enduring the unendurable."

When he finally understood that his "freeze" response was actually a survival strategy, the shame began to evaporate. He stopped seeing himself as the Victim of the started recognizing himself as the Survivor of the kidnapping.

The Hope Factor

You cannot move from Victim to Survivor without Hope.

When people come to my office for that first session, the "Intake," they are usually at rock bottom. They are anxious, depressed, and convinced they are broken.

My first job isn't to dig into the trauma. If I rip open your wounds before you have the tools to handle the pain, I am just re-traumatizing you.

My first job is to look you in the eye and say: **"I can help you with this."**

You need to believe that change is possible. You need to know that you are not permanently damaged goods. You need to know that the anxiety you feel is just your body trying to protect you, and that we can retrain it.

This is where faith often comes in. Whether you believe in God, the Universe, or just the resilience of the human spirit, you have to surrender the idea that you are in this alone. You have to trust that there is a version of you on the other side of this pain that is stronger, wiser, and whole.

I am not asking you to deny what happened. I am asking you to change the headline.

- **Old Headline:** I was attacked, and I am broken.
- **New Headline:** I was attacked, I survived, and I am still here.

Actionable Step: The Narrative Shift

We are going to start the process of moving you out of the Victim seat today. This requires confronting the story you are telling yourself.

The "It's Not My Fault" Protocol

I want you to get your journal. This is going to be uncomfortable, but we are going to do it together.

Step 1: The Event Write down the traumatic event. Keep it factual.

Who, what, where. *(e.g., "I was fired from my job unexpectedly.")*

Step 2: The Shame Script (The Victim) Write down what you are secretly blaming yourself for. What is the guilt saying? *(e.g., "I wasn't smart enough," "I should have worked harder," "I deserved it.")*

Step 3: The Reality Check (The Survivor) Now, I want you to look at that event through the eyes of a compassionate stranger. Or better yet, through the eyes of a scientist.

- Was there something out of your control?
- Did your brain/body react to protect you?
- Did someone else make a choice to hurt you?

Write the new truth: *(e.g., "The company was downsizing. My boss made a financial decision. My anxiety right now is just my brain trying to make sure I don't starve. I am talented, and I will find a new path.")*

Step 4: The Release Say this out loud: "I did the best I could with the information and resources I had at the time."

You are not guilty. You are just injured. And injuries heal.

CHAPTER 4
Anatomy of Attachment: The Invisible Operating System

We have established that you are a Survivor. You have the determination to move, and you have the purpose to guide you. But now, we have to look under the hood of the vehicle itself.

You can have the most powerful engine in the world—a heart full of ambition and a mind full of dreams—but if the steering column is broken, you are going to crash.

"No one saves us but ourselves. No one can and no one may. We ourselves must walk the path."

— **Buddha**

In the world of relationships, self-regulation, and emotional survival, that steering column is your **Attachment Style**.

I cannot tell you how many patients walk into my office, sit on my couch, and immediately start listing their "defects." They say things like, "I always pick the men who hurt me," or "I suffocate everyone I love until they leave," or "I just don't feel anything when I should feel love." They look at me with desperate eyes and say, *"Deborah, I think I'm broken."*

I look them right in the eye and tell them the first truth of the Warrior: **You are not broken. You are wired.**

There is a massive difference. If you are broken, you are trash. If you are wired, you are a person who simply needs reprogramming.

Your attachment style is the blueprint for how you connect with other human beings. It is the operating system running in the background of your brain, usually installed before you could even speak. It was written based on how your earliest caregivers—your parents or guardians—responded to your cries for help. If you don't understand this blueprint, you are destined to repeat it. A Warrior does not go into battle without understanding their own weapon.

The Core Beliefs: Your Sunglasses

Before we dissect the specific styles, we have to talk about **Core Beliefs**.

Imagine you wake up every morning and put on a pair of sunglasses. If the lenses are yellow, the whole world looks yellow. If the lenses are cracked, the whole world looks fractured.

Core beliefs are the lenses through which you interpret every single event in your life.

"What you think you become. What you feel you attract. You imagine you create."

— **Buddha**

- **The Event:** A friend doesn't text you back for four hours.
- **The Secure Lens:** "They must be busy."
- **The Insecure Lens:** "They are ignoring me. I did something wrong. They are going to leave me."

Do you see? The event (no text) is neutral. The suffering comes from the *interpretation.* These core beliefs—like "I am unlovable," "I am not good enough," or "People will always hurt me"—are the fuel for your attachment style. We have to identify the lens before we can change it.

The Four Blueprints of Connection

Psychological research generally categorizes humans into four attachment styles. I want you to read these descriptions not as a horoscope, but as a diagnostic manual. Find yourself in these pages.

The Anxious Attachment (The Pursuer)

"If I am not close to you, I am dying."

If you have this style, your nervous system is constantly scanning the horizon for abandonment. You are the person who feels a physical drop in your stomach when your partner's tone changes slightly. You are the one who double-texts, then triple-texts, then apologizes for texting.

The Wiring: Somewhere in your history, likely in childhood, love was *inconsistent.* Maybe a parent was warm one day and cold the next. Maybe they were only attentive when you were sick or achieving something. Your brain learned a hard lesson: *"Love is fragile. If I stop working for it, it will disappear."*

The Behavior: You sacrifice your own needs to keep the peace. You become a chameleon, changing your colors to match whatever you think your partner wants. You mistake anxiety for passion. When you meet someone secure—someone who is consistent and calm—you often feel bored. You think, *"There's no spark."* But what you are missing isn't the spark; it's the panic. You have been wired to believe that love requires suffering.

The Warrior's Reality Check: Your anxiety is a liar. It tells you that if you hold on tighter, you will be safe. But the truth is, you cannot squeeze water from a stone, and you cannot squeeze love from someone who doesn't want to give it. The Warrior realizes: *"I am abandoning myself to chase them."*

The Avoidant Attachment (The Distancer)

"If I let you in, you will destroy me."

For the Avoidant style, intimacy feels like a trap. You value independence above all else. When a relationship starts getting "too real"—when a partner starts asking for emotional support or commitment—you pull the ripcord. You shut down. You might be called "cold," "aloof," or "emotionally unavailable."

The Wiring: This often stems from a childhood where needs were met with rejection or annoyance. Maybe you cried, and you were told to "stop being a baby." Maybe you were left alone to self-soothe way too early. Your brain learned: *"People are unreliable. Relying on others leads to pain. The only person I can trust is me."*

The Behavior: You keep secrets. You prioritize work or hobbies over connection. You focus on your partner's flaws to justify pulling away. You look at the Anxious person and think they are "crazy" or "clingy," not realizing that your distance is triggering their anxiety, just as their pursuit is triggering your withdrawal. It is a dance of dysfunction.

The Warrior's Reality Check: You tell yourself you are independent, but often, you are just isolated. Independence is being able to stand alone. Avoidance is being *terrified* to stand together. A Warrior knows that true strength includes the courage to be vulnerable.

The Disorganized Attachment (The Chaos)

"Come here. No, get away. I need you. You terrify me."

This is the most painful style, also known as **Anxious-Avoidant**. It is often born from severe trauma or abuse. In this scenario, the person who was supposed to be your source of safety (the parent) was also the source of your fear.

The Wiring: Your brain is stuck in a biological paradox. When you are hurt, your instinct is to run *to* the caregiver. But if the caregiver *is* the threat, your brain screams "Go to them!" and "Run from them!" at the same time.

The Behavior: This results in chaotic relationships. High highs and devastating lows. You crave love desperately, but the moment you get it, you sabotage it because it feels dangerous. You might push people away and then hate them for leaving.

1. **The Secure Attachment (The Anchor)**

"I am okay, and you are okay."

This is the goal. This is where we are trying to get you. Secure attachment doesn't mean you don't have problems. It means you don't view relationship problems as a threat to your existence.

Secure people are comfortable with intimacy *and* independence. They don't panic when a partner needs space. They don't run away when a partner needs comfort. They operate from a core belief of worthiness. They assume they are lovable, so they don't need constant proof of it.

Rewiring the System: The Power of the Pause

Here is the good news, and it is the news that saves lives: **Neuroplasticity.**

Your brain is plastic. It is moldable. You are not doomed to be Anxious or Avoidant forever. You can develop what we call **"Earned Security."** You can build a Secure attachment style in adulthood, even if you didn't have one in childhood.

The shift begins with **The Pause**.

The "reptile brain," or in theory, "dorsal vagal response" (which we discussed in Chapter 3), reacts instantly. The Anxious brain sends a text before you can think. The Avoidant brain walks out of the room before you can process.

To become a Warrior, you must insert a gap between the **Trigger** and the **Reaction**.

Polyvagal Theory explains how trauma and stress affect your nervous system, influencing your ability to connect with others.

It suggests that we have an innate system for regulating emotions, which, when disrupted by early experiences, leads to attachment styles like the ones explored above. The brainstem and amygdala are involved in trauma responses, with the dorsal vagal system linked to immobilization or "freeze" reactions.

Whereas, neuroplasticity offers a solution: the brain's ability to reorganize itself by forming new neural connections in response to positive experiences, such as practicing healthy, secure connections in relationships.

This means that while your attachment style may have been wired early in life, with patience and intentional practice, you can "rewire" your brain.

You can replace old, negative thought patterns with healthier, more adaptive ones, ultimately transforming your attachment style.

The Exercise:

Next time you feel that surge of panic or that wall of ice coming up, I want you to physically stop. Put your hand on your chest. Take a breath. And ask yourself the Magic Question:

"Is this happening right now, or is this my wiring?"

- **The Scenario:** Your partner is quiet at dinner.
- **The Wiring says:** "He's mad at me. I need to fix it." (Anxious)
- **The Wiring says:** "He's boring. I need to get out of here." (Avoidant)
- **The Reality Check:** "He had a long day at work. He is tired. I am safe. I can just eat my dinner."

When you can separate the *event* from the *trauma response*, you regain control of the car. You stop driving off the cliff of your old patterns.

This is not easy work. It is the hardest work you will do. But the reward is relationships that don't hurt. The reward is peace.

CHAPTER 5
The Trap of the "Helper": Breaking the Cycle of Fawning

If you are reading this book, I am willing to bet money on something about you: You are the "Strong One."

You are the fixer. The rescuer. The reliable one. You are the person everyone calls when their car breaks down at 2:00 AM, when they are short on rent, or when they just need to dump three hours of emotional drama on someone who will listen.

You wear this "Helper" identity like a badge of honor. You think it makes you a good person. You think it makes you valuable.

But I am here to tell you the hard truth—the "Tough Love" truth that might make you angry at me: **For many trauma survivors, "Helping" is not a virtue. It is a trauma response.**

We call this **Fawning**.

"We codependents are not weak. In fact, we are as strong as steel, for others that is, but not so much for ourselves."

— **Lisa A. Romano**

The Fourth F: Fight, Flight, Freeze... and Fawn

Most people know about "Fight or Flight." We talked about "Freeze" in Chapter 3. But the fourth survival response is **Fawn**.

Fawning is when you try to avoid conflict or danger by appeasing the threat. It is "people-pleasing" on steroids.

Childhood Context: If you grew up in a volatile home—maybe with an alcoholic parent or a rage-filled caregiver—you learned that the only way to stay safe was to be useful. If you were "good," if you were "helpful," if you anticipated their needs before they even asked, maybe they wouldn't yell. Maybe they wouldn't hit.

You learned a deadly equation: **My Utility = My Safety.**

You carry this into adulthood. You attract broken people not by accident, but by design. Your subconscious seeks out "projects"—partners who are addicted, friends who are perpetually in crisis—because your wiring thinks, *"If I can fix them, I will finally be worthy. If I save them, they can't leave me."*

Enabling vs. Empowering: The Distinction

There is a razor-thin line between helping someone and hurting them. As a Warrior, you must learn the difference between **Empowering** and **Enabling**.

- **Empowering** is helping someone do something they *cannot* do for themselves.
- **Enabling** is doing something for someone that they *can and should* do for themselves.

When you enable, you are not being kind. You are being a thief. You are stealing their lesson.

If your adult son spends all his money on gambling and can't pay rent, and you pay it for him... you have just stolen his consequence. You have robbed him of the pain that might actually motivate him to change. You have taught him that his actions have no cost.

And worse, you are draining your own limited energy reserves. I want you to imagine that you have a "Life Battery" every day. It starts at 100%.

- You give 20% to your stressful job.
- You give 30% to your kids.
- You give 40% to your friend who calls to complain about the same boyfriend she refuses to break up with.

You are left with 10%. That is not enough to heal. That is not enough to build your own dreams. You are setting yourself on fire to keep other people warm, and then wondering why you are burned out.

The Sack of Stones

I want you to visualize something. Imagine you are hiking up a steep mountain. This mountain is your life. You are carrying a backpack. Inside that backpack are your own rocks—your trauma, your responsibilities, your health issues. It's heavy, but you can carry it.

Now, imagine you pass a friend on the trail. They say, "This rock is too heavy," and they hand it to you. You say, "Sure, I'll help." Then a family member hands you a boulder. Then a coworker hands you a bag of gravel.

Suddenly, you are carrying a **Sack of Stones** that doesn't belong to you. You are crushed under the weight. You can't move. And the people who gave you the stones? They are hiking up the mountain, light and free, whistling a tune.

Drop the sack.

It is not your job to carry the emotional weight of other adults. You can walk *beside* them. You can encourage them. But you cannot carry their rocks for them. A Warrior carries their own load and expects others to do the same.

The Rule of "Once"

I give my clients a simple, unbreakable rule to break the "Helper" addiction. It is called the **Rule of Once**.

- You can help someone **once**.
- You can loan them money—**once**.
- You can bail them out of a jam—**once**.
- You can listen to the same specific complaint—**once**.

The second time? It is a pattern. And if you participate in the pattern, you are no longer a Helper; you are an **Accomplice** to their dysfunction.

If a friend borrows money and doesn't pay it back, and you lend it again? You are teaching them to mistreat you. If a partner cheats, you forgive, and they cheat again? You are co-signing the behavior.

This is the hardest part of the Warrior mindset for many people. It feels mean. It feels selfish. Your guilt will scream at you.

- *Guilt says:* "You're a bad friend."
- *Warrior says:* "No. I am a healthy person refusing to participate in sickness."

Actionable Step: The Resentment Inventory

How do you know if you are enabling? **Resentment.**

Resentment is your body's way of telling you that you have overextended yourself. If you are doing something for someone—cooking dinner, loaning money, listening to a story—and you feel angry while doing it, stop immediately.

The Exercise:

1. **List the People:** Write down the names of the 3 people who drain you the most.
2. **The Favor:** What do you do for them repeatedly?
3. **The Emotion:** When you do it, do you feel happy, or do you feel used?
4. **The Verdict:** If you feel used, apply the Rule of Once. Stop doing it.

Watch what happens. The people who value *you* will understand. The people who value *what you do for them* will get angry. And that anger is the proof you needed to let them go.

CHAPTER 6
Values, Boundaries, and Self-Preservation

We have cleared the debris. We understand your wiring (Attachment). We have stopped the bleeding of energy into other people's problems (The Helper Trap). Now, we need to build the fortress.

To live as a Warrior, you need two architectural elements in your life: **A Compass (Values)** and **Walls (Boundaries).**

You cannot travel without a compass, and you cannot sleep safely without walls.

The Compass: Clarifying Your Values

In Chapter 2, we talked about Purpose as the map. Values are the compass that keeps you on the map.

A Value is not a goal. A goal is something you achieve (like "Get married"). A Value is a direction you move in (like "Being loving"). You can achieve a goal and be done with it, but you never "finish" a value.

Most of us have "Inherited Values." These are the things our parents or society told us were important.

- "You must own a home."
- "You must stay married no matter what."
- "You must be rich."

But if those values aren't *yours*, they will make you sick. When your actions do not match your true values, you feel a deep, grinding discontent. That friction is your soul screaming that you are living a lie.

"Personal freedom means having choices and no longer having to live according to someone else's authenticity."

— **Laurie Deschene**

The Values Audit: I want you to be honest. If you value **Freedom**, but you are in a controlling marriage, you will be depressed. If you value **Honesty**, but you work for a company that scams people, you will feel anxious.

You need to define your non-negotiables.

- Is it **Family**? (Then you prioritize dinner at home over overtime).
- Is it **Peace**? (Then you cut drama out of your life ruthlessly).
- Is it **Health**? (Then you do not skip your doctor's appointment for a work meeting).

The Walls: Anatomy of a Boundary

Once you know what you value, you have to protect it. That is what a boundary is.

A boundary is not a weapon. It is not an attack. It is simply a property line. It tells the world: *"This is where I end, and you begin. This is what is okay, and this is what is not okay."*

In my practice, I see boundaries on a spectrum.

1. Porous Boundaries (The Open Door) This is the "Yes" person. You overshare. You can't say no. You absorb everyone else's emotions. You are a house with no doors—anyone can walk in with muddy boots, eat your food, and sleep on your couch. You feel resentful, but you feel powerless to stop it.

2. Rigid Boundaries (The Bunker) This is the person who has been hurt so badly that they have walled themselves in. You never ask for help. You never share your feelings. You keep everyone at arm's length. You are safe, yes, but you are alone in a concrete bunker. Nothing bad gets in, but nothing good gets in either.

3. Healthy Boundaries (The Gate) This is the Warrior's way. A gate can be opened, and it can be locked. You have the agency to decide.

- "I will share my feelings with you *if* you treat me with respect."
- "I will help you *if* I have the energy."
- You decide who comes in. You decide who stays out.

The Types of Boundaries

Boundaries aren't just about saying "no." They cover every aspect of your life.

- **Physical:** Who can touch you? How close can they stand?
- **Emotional:** How much energy can someone take from you? Are you allowed to criticize me?
- **Time:** I am not available after 8:00 PM. I will not answer work emails on Sunday.
- **Material:** You cannot borrow my car. You must pay me back if I lend you money.

The "If... Then" Formula

Setting a boundary triggers fear in most survivors. We think, "If I set a boundary, they will leave." So, I am going to give you a formula that takes the emotion out of it. It is the **"If... Then" Formula**.

A boundary is useless without a consequence. "Please stop yelling" is a request. "If you yell, I will leave" is a boundary.

- *"If you continue to speak to me with that tone,* ***then*** *I will hang up the phone."*
- *"If you are more than 15 minutes late,* ***then*** *I will go into the restaurant without you."*
- *"If you drink around me,* ***then*** *I will go home."*

Notice something crucial: The "Then" is about **YOUR** action, not theirs. You cannot control them. You cannot make them stop drinking or stop yelling. You can only control *your* proximity to them.

The Extinction Burst: Expect the Pushback

I need to warn you about what happens when you start doing this. When you first set a boundary, people will not applaud you. They will not say, "Good for you, Deborah!"

They will get angry. They will push back.

In psychology, we call this an **Extinction Burst**. Think of a toddler crying for candy. If you say "No," they don't just say "Okay." They scream *louder*. They throw a tantrum. They are trying to see if the old method still works.

Your friends and family will do the same. They will say:

- "You've changed."
- "You're being selfish."
- "You're acting like a therapist."

Good. Let them scream. That pushback is proof that the boundary was necessary. It is proof that they were benefiting from your lack of boundaries.

Hold the line. If you give in during the "tantrum," you teach them that your "No" actually means "Yes, if you scream loud enough." But if you hold the line, eventually, they will adjust. They will learn the new rules of engagement. Or, they will leave.

And if they leave because you demanded respect? **Let them go.** The space they leave behind is where your new, healthy life will grow.

"Letting go gives us freedom. And freedom is the only condition for happiness."

— **Buddha**

Actionable Step: The Boundary Audit

This week, we are going to build your first gate.

1. **Identify the Leak:** Look at the three areas where you feel the most drained (Work, Family, Relationship). Where are you saying "Yes" when your gut is screaming "No"?
2. **Name the Value:** What value is being violated here? Is it your Dignity? Your Peace? Your Health?
3. **Script the Boundary:** Write down one specific "If... Then" boundary you are willing to enforce this week.

- *Example:* "value: My Sleep. Boundary: If my sister calls me after 9 PM to vent, THEN I will not answer the phone."

Write it down. Rehearse it in the mirror. Then, execute. The first time you do it, you will feel guilty. The second time, you will feel strong. The third time, you will be free.

CHAPTER 7

The Art of Detachment: The Warrior's Shield

We have spent the first half of this book in the trenches. We have looked at your trauma, dissected your attachment style, and audited your boundaries. We have been doing the heavy lifting of *awareness*.

Now, we move into the **Warrior's Wisdom**.

If there is one skill that separates the Survivor from the Warrior, it is **Detachment**.

When I say "Detachment," most people recoil. They think I mean becoming cold, unfeeling, or indifferent. They think it means sitting on a mountaintop, ignoring the world. That is not detachment. That is dissociation.

True Detachment is not the absence of emotion. It is the absence of manipulation.

It is the radical, terrifying, and liberating realization that you can do everything right—you can love perfectly, work hardest, and pray loudest—and you still cannot control the outcome. The Victim fights reality. The Warrior accepts reality, and in that acceptance, finds the strategy to win.

The War of the Outcome

I want to share a story that is very close to my heart. It is a story about my sister, and it is the story of how I learned that love alone is not enough to save people.

My sister is a beautiful, intelligent woman. But like many of us, she had a "broken picker." She fell in love with a man who was, to put it lightly, a nightmare. He was controlling. He was manipulative. He was a professional wrestler—a big, physically imposing guy—and he used that size to intimidate her.

I saw the red flags immediately. I saw the way he talked to her. I saw the way she shrank when he walked into the room.

For two years, I made it my full-time job to "save" her. I would spend two hours on the phone with her every night. She would call me crying, telling me what he did, and I would go into "Crisis Manager" mode. *"You have to leave him." "Here is a plan." "He is dangerous. Get out now."*

I was pouring my life force into her. I was losing sleep. I was stressed. My own life was put on hold because I was so consumed by *her* crisis. I thought, *"If I just explain it clearly enough, she will leave. If I just love her enough, she will see the light."*

And you know what happened? Nothing. She stayed. In fact, the more I pushed, the more she defended him.

Then came the escalation. He became violent. He started threatening us. He started stalking us. It got to the point where I had to tell her, *"You have to leave, or I have to walk away. Because he is going to kill you, and I cannot watch it happen."*

She didn't leave. So, I did.

I detached. I told her, *"I love you. But I cannot participate in this anymore. If you ever decide to leave, I will be here with a moving truck in five minutes. But until then, I cannot hear about him. I cannot fix this."*

It was the hardest thing I have ever done. It felt like I was abandoning her in a burning building. But here is the truth: **I wasn't holding her up. I was just drowning with her.**

Months later, when the pain became too great for *her*, she finally left him. She saved herself. My lectures didn't save her. Her own survival instinct saved her.

That experience taught me the core tenet of Eastern Wisdom: **The root of suffering is attachment to the outcome.**

I was suffering because I was attached to the outcome of "saving her." I believed I had control over another human being's choices. I didn't. Once I released the outcome—once I accepted that she might stay, and she might even die—I regained my power. I stopped bleeding energy. And when she *did* finally call for help, I was strong enough to answer.

The Illusion of Permanence

In the West, we are obsessed with "Forever." We want the "Forever Home." The "Forever Marriage." We want our health to stay perfect forever. We want our children to stay safe forever.

But if you look at nature—or if you just look in the mirror—you see the undeniable truth: **Nothing is permanent.**

I am older now. I look at my hands, and they are different from what they were at 20. I look at my life, and the people who were my "entire world" ten years ago are gone, replaced by new people.

The Victim looks at change and calls it a Tragedy. The Warrior looks at change and calls it a Season.

When you fight impermanence, you lose. You cannot stop the waves from crashing on the shore. You can stand there and scream at the ocean, "Stop moving!" and you will drown. Or, you can learn to surf.

Detachment is the surfboard. It is the understanding that:

- This job might not last forever.
- This relationship might not last forever.
- This pain will not last forever.

When you embrace the fact that everything is temporary, you stop gripping your life so tightly. You stop living in the anxiety of *"What if I lose it?"* and start living in the presence of *"I have it now."*

The Pilot, The Plane, and The Engineer

So, how do we actually *do* this? How do we care about our lives without being destroyed by the anxiety of control?

I use a metaphor with my clients that I call **The Aviation Triad**. To fly a plane successfully, you need three distinct roles. In your life, you must play all three, but you must know *which* one you are playing at any given moment.

1. The Pilot (Values & Direction)

The Pilot's job is simple: Set the course. The Pilot looks at the map and says, *"We are going to Paris."* The Pilot does not fly the plane. The Pilot does not fix the engine. The Pilot simply holds the **Intention**.

In your life, this is your **Purpose** (Chapter 2). *"I am going to be a healthy person." "I am going to build a career in art." "I am going to leave this abusive marriage."*

2. The Plane (The Vehicle)

The Plane is the machine. It is your body, your subconscious mind, and the circumstances of your life. The Plane encounters turbulence. It hits storms. It gets tossed around by the wind. If the Pilot tries to micro-manage every bolt and screw while the plane is flying, the plane crashes. The Pilot has to **Trust the Plane** to do what it was designed to do—fly.

3. The Engineer (The Detached Fixer)

This is the most important role for the Warrior. When a red light flashes on the dashboard—say, an engine light comes on—the Pilot doesn't scream, *"Oh my god, I'm a failure! Why does the plane hate me? I'm unlovable!"*

No. The Pilot calls the Engineer. The Engineer looks at the red light and says, *"Hmm. Low oil pressure. Interesting."* The Engineer is **Detached**. The Engineer doesn't take the broken part personally. They just assess the data and apply the fix.

The Problem with Trauma Survivors: Trauma survivors confuse these roles. When you hit a bump in life (The Plane hits turbulence), you panic. You abandon the cockpit. You start running around the cabin screaming. You take the turbulence personally. *"Why is this happening to me? I must be bad. I'm being punished."*

- **The Warrior's Approach:** When things go wrong—and they

will—you switch to the Engineer.

- **Event:** You lose your job.
- **Victim Response:** "I am a failure. I'll never work again."
- **Warrior (Engineer) Response:** "Red light on the dashboard. Cash flow has stopped. Okay. What is the protocol? Update resume. Cut expenses. Apply to 5 jobs a day."

Do you see the difference? The Engineer doesn't cry over the broken part. The Engineer fixes it. That is detachment. It is taking the emotion out of the mechanics of survival.

Radical Acceptance: The "So What?" Factor

This leads us to the most powerful tool in the Warrior's arsenal: **Radical Acceptance.**

Radical Acceptance is not approval. It doesn't mean you *like* the situation. It means you stop arguing with the fact that the situation is happening.

We cannot change anything unless we accept it. Condemnation does not liberate; it oppresses."

— **C.G. Jung**

I have clients who spend years arguing with reality. *"He shouldn't have cheated on me." "My mother shouldn't have been so cruel." "I shouldn't have gotten sick."*

You are right. They shouldn't have. But they **did**. As long as you are stuck in "should," you are trapped in the past. You are arguing with a tombstone.

Radical Acceptance is looking at the wreckage and saying, **"This happened. Now what?"**

I learned this when I had my strokes. I was young. I was healthy. I shouldn't have had a stroke. It wasn't fair. I could have spent the next ten years bitter, asking God why he did this to me. I could have stayed in bed, mourning the body I used to have.

Instead, I used Radical Acceptance. *"Okay. I had a stroke. My brain is different now. My energy is different now. This is the new terrain."* Once I accepted it, I could work *with* it. I adjusted my schedule. I prioritized my sleep. I changed my diet. I built a life that worked for *this* version of Deborah, not the version that existed before.

"No Guts, No Glory." This acceptance allows you to take risks. I tell my clients all the time: **No Guts, No Glory.**

If you are terrified of a negative outcome, you will never try.

- You won't ask for the promotion because they *might* say no.
- You won't ask that person out because they *might* reject you.

But when you practice Detachment, you realize: *"If they say no, I will survive. If they reject me, I will survive."* You detach from the fear of the "No." You realize that "No" is just data. It's just a red light on the dashboard. It doesn't mean you are broken; it just means you need to turn the plane in a different direction.

Trusting the Flow: The Farmer and the Horse

There is an old Eastern parable that perfectly illustrates this mindset.

A farmer had a beautiful horse. One day, the horse ran away. The neighbors came by and said, *"This is terrible! What bad luck."* The farmer simply said, **"Maybe."**

The next day, the horse returned, bringing three wild horses with it. The neighbors exclaimed, *"This is amazing! What good luck."* The farmer said, **"Maybe."**

The next day, the farmer's son tried to ride one of the wild horses, fell off, and broke his leg. The neighbors said, *"This is a tragedy! What bad luck."* The farmer said, **"Maybe."**

The next day, the army came to the village to draft all the young men for the war. They passed over the farmer's son because his leg was broken. All the other sons died in the war. The farmer's son lived.

The Lesson: You do not know if an event is "good" or "bad" when it happens. You only see one frame of the movie.

- My sister leaving her husband seemed like a tragedy to her at the time—she was heartbroken. But it was the beginning of her freedom.
- My strokes seemed like a disaster. But they gave me the empathy and the "No Losses" philosophy that allowed me to write this book and help thousands of people.

When you detach, you stop judging every moment as a catastrophe. You lean back. You let the movie play out. You trust that even the dark scenes are moving the plot forward.

Actionable Step: The "Outcome Release" Visualization

We are going to practice being the Pilot and the Engineer, but letting go of the turbulence.

The Exercise:

1. **Identify the Struggle:** Write down the one situation in your life right now where you are desperately trying to control the outcome. (e.g., "Making my partner change," "Getting a specific job," "Fixing a family member").
2. **The Worst-Case Scenario:** I want you to go to the dark place. If you *don't* get what you want, what happens?
   - *If he leaves me... I will be alone.*
   - *If I don't get the job... I will be broke.*
3. **The Engineer's Assessment:** Look at that worst-case scenario. Is it fatal?
   - *Are you dead?* No.
   - *Can you survive being alone?* Yes. You did it before you met him.

- *Can you survive being broke?* Yes. You can get a different job. You can downsize.

4. **The Release:** Close your eyes. Visualize that outcome you are gripping so tightly—that relationship, that job. Imagine it is a rope you are holding in your hands. Your knuckles are white. It hurts. Now, imagine opening your hands. Watch the rope drift away. Say out loud: **"I release the outcome. I trust the flow. Whatever happens, I will handle it."**

Feel the weight lift off your shoulders. That is the feeling of the Warrior putting down the shield, not because the war is over, but because she knows she doesn't need to fight *everything* to survive. She only needs to fly the plane.

CHAPTER 8
Facing Fear and Rewiring the Brain

We have arrived at the threshold.

In the previous chapter, we learned the Art of Detachment—how to stop gripping the outcome so tight that your knuckles bleed. Now, we must address the invisible force that makes us grip that outcome in the first place.

Fear.

If Detachment is the shield, then Courage is the sword. And you cannot wield the sword if you are paralyzed by the fear of what *might* happen.

I tell my clients this truth often, and it usually makes them uncomfortable: **Safety is an illusion.**

We spend our entire lives trying to build walls of safety. We stay in the job we hate because it is "safe." We stay in a mediocre relationship because being alone feels "unsafe." We don't write the book, start the business, or set the boundary because we are terrified of the risk.

But here is the biological reality: **Nothing in nature is static.** Your cells are dying and regenerating every second. The seasons change. The economy shifts. The people you love will eventually leave or die.

You can hide in your basement, wrapped in bubble wrap, and life will still find you.

The Survivor tries to stay safe. The Warrior accepts that safety is impossible and chooses **Growth** instead.

The Growth Choice: No Guts, No Glory

There is a phrase I use in my practice that sums up the entire philosophy of recovery: **No Guts, No Glory.**

It sounds like a bumper sticker, but it is deeply clinical. You cannot achieve emotional maturity without risk.

- If you want deep intimacy, you must risk deep heartbreak.
- If you want professional success, you must risk public failure.
- If you want to heal, you must risk feeling the pain you have been repressing for twenty years.

Many of my clients come to me because they are "stuck." They feel stagnant. They say, "Deborah, I'm just not moving forward." I ask them, "What risks have you taken in the last year?" Usually, the answer is *none.*

They are waiting for the fear to go away before they act. They are waiting to feel "ready." I have to break the bad news: **You will never feel ready.** The fear does not vanish. You just decide that the *Glory* (the life you want) is more important than the *Gut* (the fear you feel).

You have to make the **Growth Choice**. In every moment, you have two options: Step forward into growth, or step backward into safety. Stepping forward triggers anxiety. Stepping backward triggers depression. Pick your poison. A Warrior picks the anxiety of growth over the depression of stagnation every single time.

Escaping Time: The Trap of Past and Future

Fear lives in time. Specifically, fear lives in the future. Depression lives in the past. Peace? Peace only lives in the **Now**.

I see this split in my office every day.

- **The Depressed Client:** They are ruminating. They are replaying the tape of their abuse, their divorce, their failures. They are trying to change a history that is already written in stone.
- **The Anxious Client:** They are "future-tripping." They are obsessed with the "What Ifs." *What if I get fired? What if he leaves? What if I get sick?*

Both of them are missing their actual life.

The Lesson of Control (The COVID Reality Check) If there is one thing recent history taught us, it is that control is a myth. Look at COVID. In 2019, we all had our five-year plans. We had our vacations booked. We thought we knew exactly what the future held. Snap your fingers. The world stopped. Jobs vanished. Schools closed. People we loved were suddenly gone.

It was a brutal lesson, but a necessary one. It taught us that we **never** had control. We only had the *illusion* of control.

When you spend your energy trying to predict the future to avoid pain, you are wasting your life battery on a hallucination. You cannot know what is coming. You could walk out of your house today and win the lottery, or you could get hit by a bus.

The Warrior understands: **I can only handle Today.** I can handle this hour. I can handle this breath. If I project myself ten years into the future, I will collapse under the weight of imaginary problems. But if I stay right here, in this room, in this body? I am usually okay.

Neuroplasticity: You Are Not Hardwired

Now, let's get into the science of *how* we change. For a long time, psychology believed that once you were an adult, your brain was set. You were who you were. If you were anxious, you stayed anxious. We now know that is false.

The brain is **Plastic**. It is malleable. It changes based on what you *do* and what you *think*. This is called **Neuroplasticity**.

My Stroke of Insight – I don't just know this from textbooks. I know this from my own brain. When I had my strokes, parts of my brain died. Literal tissue death. Functions I took for granted—movement, speech—were damaged. If the brain was static, I would have stayed that way. But the brain is a miracle. Through rehab, through repetition, through doing the same exercises thousands of times, my brain rewired itself. It built new neural pathways to bypass the damaged areas. It said, *"Okay, that road is closed? We will build a new highway."*

The Mental Groove – Your thoughts work the same way. If you have spent 20 years thinking, *"I am stupid,"* or *"I am unlovable,"* you have dug a deep, paved highway in your brain. That thought is the path of least resistance. When something goes wrong, your brain automatically zooms down the "I am stupid" highway because it is fast and easy.

To change, we have to build a new road. And just like my physical rehab, it requires Repetition. You cannot just think a positive thought once. You have to think it ten thousand times. You have to force your brain, over and over, to take the new path until the old path gets overgrown with weeds.

The Tool: Socratic Questioning

How do we actually do this? We can't just lie to ourselves. If you feel like a failure, standing in the mirror and saying "I am a success" feels like a lie. Your brain rejects it.

We need a tool that respects your intelligence. That tool is **Socratic Questioning**.

Socrates didn't tell people what to think. He asked them questions until they realized their thinking was flawed. We are going to do the same thing to your inner critic.

The Scenario: Let's say you made a mistake at work. **The Automatic Thought:** *"I am a total failure."*

Most people stop there. They accept that thought as a Fact. The Warrior puts that thought on trial.

Step 1: Examine the Evidence: Is it true that you are a *total* failure? Let's look at the data.

- Are you a failure at brushing your teeth? No.
- Are you a failure at feeding your dog? No.
- Are you a failure at being a friend? No.

Did you fail at *every* task at work today, or just this one? Just this one.

Step 2: Calculate the Percentage: I love numbers because numbers don't have feelings. If you made one mistake in a day where you did 50 things right, what is your failure percentage? Maybe 2%. So, you were a success 98% of the time.

To call yourself a "Total Failure" based on 2% data is statistically inaccurate. It is a lie.

Step 3: The Replacement Thought: Now, we replace the irrational thought with a **Rational Response**. We don't say, *"I am perfect."* That's toxic positivity. We say: *"I am a competent person who made a mistake in 2% of my day. I can fix it and move on."*

Do you feel the difference? The first thought ("I am a failure") triggers shame and depression. The second thought ("I made a 2% error") triggers problem-solving.

This is how you rewire the brain. You catch the lie. You examine the evidence. You replace it with the truth. And you do it every single day.

The 80/20 Rule of Self-Worth

I want to give you a benchmark for self-worth. Perfection is not the goal. Perfection is a trauma response. The goal is the **80/20 Rule**.

If you are getting it right 80% of the time, you are winning. If you are a good parent 80% of the time, and you lose your temper 20% of the time? You are a good parent. If you eat healthy 80% of the time? You are healthy.

Trauma survivors zoom in on the 20%. They obsess over the mistake. They obsess over the awkward conversation. They obsess over the one pound they gained. They ignore the 80% of success.

Your job, starting today, is to widen the lens. You have to force your brain to acknowledge the 80%. *"Look, I paid my bills." "Look, I was kind to the barista." "Look, I didn't text my toxic ex."*

That is evidence. Collect it. Hoard it. Use it to pave that new highway in your mind.

Actionable Step: The Thought Court

We are going to put your inner critic on trial this week.

The Exercise:

Catch the Thought: Keep a small notebook or use the notes app on your phone. Whenever you feel a sudden drop in mood (shame, anxiety, hopelessness), stop. Ask: *"What was I just thinking?"* Write it down. (e.g., *"He didn't call. He must hate me."*)

The Cross-Examination: Ask these three questions against that thought:

- *Is this 100% true?* (Can I prove he hates me? Or is he just busy?)
- *What is the evidence AGAINST this thought?* (He told me he loved me yesterday. He has a busy job.)
- *Is this thought helpful?* (Does thinking this help me, or does it paralyze me?)

The Verdict (The Rewrite): Write a new, fact-based sentence.

- *"He hasn't called yet. I don't know why. I know he is busy. I am worthy of love regardless of when the phone rings. I will go on with my day."*

Do this for one week. You will be shocked at how many lies you tell yourself in a 24-hour period. And you will be amazed at how powerful you feel when you start talking back.

You are not your thoughts. You are the Thinker of your thoughts. Take the wheel.

CHAPTER 9
The Power of Self-Compassion: Dropping the Sack of Stones

We are nearing the summit of your journey.

You have learned to reframe your trauma as lessons. You have identified your attachment style and learned to set boundaries. You have even begun the terrifying work of rewiring your brain to face fear. You are doing the work of a Warrior.

But I have noticed something in my practice. A patient can do all the "homework"—they can journal, they can meditate, they can face their fears—and yet, they still look tired. They still walk with a heaviness, a slump in their shoulders, a dullness in their eyes.

I ask them, *"Why are you so tired?"* They say, *"I don't know. I'm fighting so hard, but I feel like I'm dragging something behind me."*

They are right. They are dragging something. They are hiking up the mountain of recovery, but they have not yet done the one thing that makes the climb possible.

They haven't dropped the **Sack of Stones**.

The Anatomy of the Sack

I want you to close your eyes for a moment. Imagine that on your back, there is a burlap sack. It is old, it is frayed, and it is heavy. Inside that sack are stones. Some are small pebbles. Some are jagged rocks. Some are massive boulders that threaten to crush your spine.

What are these stones? They are your **Resentments**. They are your **Grudges**. They are the **"Should Haves"** and the **"Could Haves."**

- *That stone right there?* That is the anger you feel toward your father for not protecting you.

- *That sharp one?* That is the hatred you feel toward your ex-husband for leaving you for a younger woman.
- *That heavy boulder at the bottom?* That is the shame you feel toward *yourself* for staying too long, for not being smarter, for not being stronger.

We carry these sacks everywhere we go. We take them to work. We take them into new relationships. We take them to bed at night. We think that carrying them is necessary. We think, *"If I put this stone down, it means I forgive him. If I put this stone down, it means what happened to me was okay."*

So, we grip the sack tighter. We let the straps dig into our skin. We bleed. And we call this "strength."

I am here to tell you the most liberating truth of your life: **Carrying the stone does not hurt the person who threw it. It only hurts you.**

Holding onto resentment is like drinking poison and waiting for the other person to die. The person who hurt you? They are likely sleeping soundly. They are hiking up their own mountain, unencumbered. Meanwhile, you are sweating, bleeding, and collapsing under the weight of a past that cannot be changed.

It is time to drop the sack.

The Myth of "Toughness"

Before we can drop the sack, we have to talk about how we treat the person carrying it.

Trauma survivors are often the harshest critics on the planet. We believe that the way to fix ourselves is to beat ourselves into submission. We look in the mirror and say: *"You're so stupid for letting that happen." "Why aren't you over this yet?" "You're weak." "Look at you, crying again. Pathetic."*

We think this is "discipline." We think this is how we force ourselves to get better. But let me ask you a question.

Imagine a bird with a broken wing. It is lying on the ground, struggling, in pain. Would you walk up to that bird and kick it? Would you scream at it, *"Get up! Fly! Why is your wing broken, you idiot?"*

Of course not. That would be cruel. It would be insane. You know that kicking a bird with a broken wing doesn't fix the wing; it kills the bird. To heal the wing, you need gentleness. You need a splint. You need rest. You need protection.

You are the bird with the broken wing.

Trauma is an injury. It is not a character defect. When you berate yourself for your trauma responses—for your anxiety, your fear, your "freeze" moments—you are kicking the broken wing. You are adding secondary trauma to the original wound.

This brings us to the concept of **Self-Compassion**. Now, I know the Warriors reading this might roll their eyes. "Compassion" sounds soft. It sounds like giving up. It is the opposite. Self-compassion is the hardest, bravest thing you will ever do. It is the refusal to be your own abuser.

If you wouldn't say it to your best friend, you are not allowed to say it to yourself. If your best friend came to you and said, *"I'm having a panic attack,"* would you say, *"You're so dramatic, shut up"*? No. You would say, *"It's okay. Breathe. I'm here."*

Be your own friend. That is how the wing heals.

The Art of Eviction (Forgiveness)

To drop the Sack of Stones, we have to talk about the "F" word: **Forgiveness.**

I have had clients almost walk out of my office when I use that word. *"Deborah, you don't understand what he did to me. It is unforgivable."*

I stop them right there. **Forgiveness is not about them.** Forgiveness does not mean reconciliation. It does not mean what they did was acceptable. It does not mean you have to invite them to Thanksgiving dinner.

Forgiveness is simply **Eviction**.

Right now, the person who hurt you is living rent-free in your head. They are taking up space in your thoughts. They are consuming your emotional energy. Every time you replay the argument, every time you fantasize about revenge, every time you check their social media to see if they are happy... you are paying their rent.

Forgiveness is serving them an eviction notice. It is saying: *"You don't live here anymore. I need this space for my joy. I need this energy for my dreams. I am taking my house back."*

When you drop the stone of resentment, you are not saying, *"It didn't hurt."* You are saying, *"It hurts less than holding onto it forever."*

The Empty Well: Shifting to Internal Validation

Why is it so hard to drop the stones? Usually, it is because we are waiting for something. We are waiting for an apology. We are waiting for closure. We are waiting for them to admit they were wrong.

We are standing at a dry well, dropping bucket after bucket down, hoping that *this time*, it will come up with water.

- *If I just explain it one more time, my mother will finally understand.*
- *If I just achieve enough, my father will finally be proud.*
- *If I just suffer enough, the universe will settle the score.*

The well is dry. There is no water down there. And as long as you are standing at that well, waiting for external validation, you are dying of thirst.

The ultimate goal of the Warrior—the shift that changes everything—is realizing that **Happiness is an Inside Job**.

If your happiness depends on external circumstances—on the weather, on the stock market, on your partner's mood, on an apology—then you are a slave to those circumstances. You are a leaf blowing in the wind. But if your happiness comes from your own sense of worth, your own integrity, your own resilience? Then you are the mountain. The wind can blow, the rain can fall, but the mountain does not move.

You have to stop asking the person who broke you to put you back together. They don't have the pieces. Only you have the pieces.

The Lightness of Being

I want to tell you what happens when you finally drop the sack.

I remember when I did it. I had been carrying resentment toward my family for the way they treated me when I was sick—the "Sack of Stones" of abandonment I told you about in Chapter 2. For years, I carried it. I used it as armor. *"Look how much I survived. Look how alone I was."* It made me feel strong, but it also made me hard.

One day, I realized: *This anger is boring.* It wasn't protecting me anymore; it was just weighing me down. It was keeping me connected to people I didn't even like.

So, I dropped it. I didn't call them and tell them. I didn't make a big scene. I just... let go of the rope. I decided that their behavior was about *them*, and my peace was about *me.*

The feeling was instant. It was **Lightness**. It felt like I could take a full breath for the first time in years. My step was bouncier. My laughter was louder. The energy I had been using to keep the "Shield of Anger" up was suddenly available for other things—for writing, for helping clients, for loving the people who *did* show up for me.

This is the promise I make to you: **On the other side of forgiveness is Freedom.**

When you stop wasting energy on the past, you become dangerous in the best way possible. You become a creator. You become powerful. You become a Warrior who fights for the future, not a Victim who fights the past.

Self-Care: The Practice of Replenishment

Self-care is not just about bubble baths or occasional indulgences. It is about the deeper, everyday practices that replenish your spirit and restore your strength. Think of self-care as you would think of caring for a pet. If you've ever had a dog, you know how they offer unconditional love, how their simple presence teaches patience and brings joy. The act of petting them, caring for them, and just being with them shows you the beauty of nurturing and being nurtured.

Self-compassion is like that: loving yourself unconditionally, giving yourself the grace to heal. This can come in many forms: journaling your thoughts, dancing in your living room to your favorite song, exercising to release pent-up energy, or simply spending time with loved ones who fill you with joy. You are learning how to love yourself again after hardship, to be gentle with yourself as you would be with a beloved pet.

"Sometimes self-care is exercise and eating right. Sometimes it's spending time with loved ones or taking a nap. And sometimes it's watching an entire season of TV in one weekend while you lounge around in your pajamas. Whatever soothes your soul."

— **Nanea Hoffman**

Actionable Step: The Release Ceremony

We are going to do something physical today to symbolize this internal shift. You cannot just "think" your way out of resentment; sometimes you have to act your way out.

The "Release Letter" Protocol

Step 1: The Audit: I want you to identify the heaviest stone in your sack. Who are you most angry at? Who have you not forgiven? (It might be yourself).

Step 2: The Letter: Write a letter to this person. **Do not hold back.** This is for your eyes only. Write down everything they did. Write down how much it hurt. Scream on the paper. Cry on the paper. Use the foulest language you know. Get every ounce of poison out of your system and onto the page. Then, write this sentence at the end: *"I have carried this for long enough. It is too heavy, and it is not mine. I am giving it back to you. I am done."*

Step 3: The Destruction: Do not send this letter. Sending it is an attempt to get a reaction (standing at the dry well). Instead, destroy it. Burn it safely in a sink or fire pit. Shred it. Tear it into tiny pieces and flush it. As you watch it burn or disappear, visualize that stone rolling off your back and tumbling down the mountain.

Step 4: The Affirmation: Stand up tall. Roll your shoulders back. Take a deep breath. Say out loud: **"I am light. I am free. I am whole."**

You have dropped the weight. Now, look up. The summit is right there. And you have the energy to reach it.

CHAPTER 10
Compassion, Freedom, and the Warrior's Life

We have climbed a long way together.

Look back at where we started. We began in the mud of the "Victim" mindset, where life was something that happened *to* you. We moved through the grit of the "Survivor" mindset, where you learned to grit your teeth and endure.

But now, we stand at the precipice of something greater. We are stepping into the identity of the **Warrior**.

I want to pause here and redefine that word, because "Warrior" often conjures images of battles, shields, and bloodshed. In the context of this book—and your life—a Warrior is not someone who is constantly fighting. A Warrior is someone who has found **Peace**.

A Victim fights reality because they feel persecuted by it. A Survivor fights reality because they are terrified of it. A Warrior *accepts* reality, masters their response to it, and finds freedom in the midst of it.

This chapter is about that Freedom. It is about the "Conqueror" mindset—the state of being where your happiness is no longer hostage to your circumstances.

The Compassion Paradox

In the last chapter, we dropped the Sack of Stones. We talked about Self-Compassion. I want to deepen that concept because it is the fuel for the Warrior's life.

There is a misconception that "Compassion" is soft. We think of it as a warm, fuzzy blanket. But in my practice, and in my own life recovering from strokes and trauma, I have found that Compassion is actually **Titanium**.

Think about it. What requires more strength: To scream at yourself when you make a mistake? Or to take a breath, look in the mirror, and say, *"I am human. I am learning. I will try again."*

The first reaction is reactive; it's the reptile brain lashing out. The second reaction requires conscious control, emotional regulation, and deep wisdom.

Compassion is the armor that protects you from the world's negativity. When you are truly compassionate toward yourself, the insults of others bounce off you.

- If someone calls you "stupid," but you *know* and *accept* your own intelligence and value, their words have no sticky surface to cling to.
- If someone rejects you, but you have not rejected *yourself*, you remain whole.

The Warrior knows that the relationship they have with themselves is the blueprint for every other relationship in their life. If you treat yourself with dignity, you will unconsciously demand it from others. You won't have to scream for respect; you will simply embody it.

The Ultimate Goal: The Inside Job

This brings us to the core secret of the Warrior's Life, the "Holy Grail" that every therapy patient is searching for.

Happiness is an Inside Job.

I know, I know. You've heard it on Instagram quotes. But I want you to really feel the weight of it. Most of us live our lives as "Externalists." We believe our internal state is dependent on external variables.

- *"I will be happy when I get the promotion."*
- *"I will be calm when my kids behave."*
- *"I will be secure when I have $50,000 in the bank."*

- *"I will be worthy when he apologizes."*

This is a trap. It is a recipe for anxiety because you cannot control any of those variables. You are handing the remote control of your emotions to your boss, your kids, the economy, and your ex.

The Warrior takes the remote control back.

The Conqueror Mindset says: *"I am happy not because everything is perfect, but because I have decided to be." "I am calm not because the storm has passed, but because I am the shelter."*

I remember a specific moment in my own recovery. I was still dealing with the physical aftershocks of my health issues. My bank account wasn't where I wanted it to be. My life looked nothing like the "perfect picture" I had imagined at 20. But I sat on my porch, drank my coffee, and felt a wave of joy so potent it almost brought me to my knees.

Nothing outside had changed. But *I* had changed. I realized I wasn't waiting for permission to be happy anymore. I wasn't waiting for the "loss" to be fixed. I had found the lesson, and in the lesson, I found gratitude. That is the moment the Warrior emerges when you can look at an imperfect life and feel perfect peace.

Freedom is a Verb

So, what does this Freedom look like in practice? It looks like **Detachment with Love** (as we discussed in Chapter 7), but applied to your entire existence.

1. Freedom from the Past The Warrior visits the past like a library. You go there to learn, to reference a lesson, or to appreciate how far you've come. But you don't *live* in the library. You don't sleep in the aisles. You take the wisdom, and you walk back out into the sunlight of the present.

2. Freedom from Other People's Opinions This is the big one. When you are a Victim, you are terrified of what "They" think. When you are a Survivor, you are defensive about what "They" think. When you are a Warrior, you are curious but indifferent to what "They" think.

You realize that people view you through the lens of their own trauma, their own values, and their own limitations.

- If they call you "selfish" for setting a boundary, you recognize that it is *their* reaction to losing access to you. It is not a fact about your character.
- If they judge your path, you realize they are judging it from the map of *their* life, not yours.

This freedom allows you to be authentic. You stop performing. You stop shapeshifting to fit into rooms that are too small for you. You walk into a room as *You*—scars, lessons, humor, weirdness, and all—and you are okay if some people don't get it. The Warrior would rather be rejected for who they are than accepted for who they are not.

3. Freedom from the "Shoulds" We torture ourselves with "Shoulds." *"I should be married by now." "I should be further along in my career." "I should be over this grief."*

The Warrior replaces "Should" with "Is." *"I am single. And I am building a life I love." "I am exactly where I am. And I am moving forward." "I am sad today. And that is okay."*

When you stop arguing with reality, you free up so much energy. You stop wasting your life wishing it was different and start actually *living* the one you have.

The View from the Summit

I want you to imagine that mountain we've been climbing. You are at the top now. Look down.

See that dark valley where you started? That was the trauma. That was the loss. See the steep, rocky path? That was the struggle. That was the determination. See the plateaus where you rested? Those were the moments of insight.

From up here, it all looks different. You don't see the mud on your boots anymore. You see the view. You see that the valley was necessary to carve out the depth of your character. You see that the steep climb gave you muscles that people who took the easy road don't have.

You realize that **No Loss was wasted.** Every tear watered a seed. Every scar is a map. Every heartbreak expanded your capacity to love.

You are not "damaged goods." You are a masterpiece forged in fire. The Japanese have an art form called *Kintsugi*, where they repair broken pottery with gold lacquer. They don't hide the cracks; they highlight them. They believe the piece is *more* beautiful for having been broken.

You are the Kintsugi. Your cracks are where the gold is. Your wisdom, your empathy, your resilience—that is the gold that shines through the places where life tried to break you.

Integrating the Warrior

As we prepare to move into the final chapter—the practical guide to living this every day—I want you to make a vow to yourself.

This isn't a vow to be perfect. This isn't a vow to never feel sad, or scared, or angry again. Warriors feel all of that. This is a vow to never abandon yourself again.

Stand up (physically, do it right now). Put your hand on your heart. Feel that rhythm? That is the drumbeat of survival. That is the engine that kept you going when you wanted to quit. Say this out loud:

"I am not what happened to me. I am what I choose to become." "I release the need to be saved, because I have learned to save myself." "I am the Warrior of my own life."

Feel that shift? That lightness in your chest? That is Freedom. That is the sack of stones rolling down the hill. That is the "Conqueror" waking up.

You have done the hard work. You have faced the darkness. Now, it is time to turn your face toward the sun and simply... live.

Actionable Step: The "Conqueror" Manifesto

We are going to solidify this shift with a declaration.

1. Write Your Manifesto: I want you to write 5 "I Am" statements that define your new identity. These should contradict your old "Victim" beliefs.

- *Old Belief:* I am broken. -> **Warrior Truth:** *I am rebuilding stronger.*
- *Old Belief:* I am alone. -> **Warrior Truth:** *I am my own best company, and I attract healthy love.*
- *Old Belief:* I am afraid of the future. -> **Warrior Truth:** *I trust myself to handle whatever comes.*

2. The Mirror Work: Tape this list to your bathroom mirror. Every morning, before you look at your phone or check your email, look yourself in the eye and read them out loud. This is how we continue the neuroplasticity work. We are programming the GPS for "Freedom."

3. The Celebration: Do one thing today just because it makes you happy. Not because it's productive. Not because it helps someone else. Eat the cake. Buy the flowers. Take a nap. Celebrate the fact that you are still here, and you are free.

CHAPTER 11
Living the Warrior's Life: The Everyday Revolution

We have reached the final stage of our journey.

You have traveled from the disempowerment of the Victim, through the gritty endurance of the Survivor, and arrived at the sovereign ground of the Warrior. But a Warrior is not a statue. A Warrior is a living, breathing force. The title isn't a trophy you put on a shelf; it is a way of walking through the world.

The question I get most often from clients as they graduate from therapy is: *"Deborah, how do I keep this up? How do I stay a Warrior when the world is still chaotic, when my family is still crazy, and when I still have bad days?"*

The answer is simple, but it is not easy. **You don't do it all at once. You do it every single day.**

Being a Warrior isn't about slaying a dragon once a year. It is about the quiet, consistent revolution of your daily choices. It is about how you wake up, how you treat yourself when you drop your coffee, how you speak to your friend, and how you close your eyes at night.

The Anchor of Purpose

In a world that feels like it is on fire—with wars, political division, and chaos on the news every night—it is easy to feel small. It is easy to feel helpless.

When I look at the state of the world, I don't despair. I go back to my **Purpose**. As I told you in the recording of my own life, my purpose has evolved. It used to be just surviving. Then it was helping my clients one-on-one. Now, it is reaching a bigger audience—writing this book, doing the TV show—because I know that if I can help *you* heal, you will go out and heal your family, and that ripple effect is how we change the world.

The Everyday Warrior knows their "Why." When the alarm goes off, and you want to pull the covers over your head, your Purpose is what pulls you out of bed.

- *"I am getting up because I am breaking the cycle of trauma for my children."*
- *"I am going to work because I am building a life of financial freedom."*
- *"I am setting this boundary because I am teaching the world how to treat me."*

If you don't have a purpose, you will drift. And when you drift, you eventually crash into the rocks of your old habits. Keep your purpose in your pocket. Touch it every day.

Boundaries: The Architecture of Freedom

If Purpose is the engine, **Boundaries** are the steering wheel. We talked about boundaries in Chapter 6, but now I want to talk about them as a lifestyle.

The most profound realization you will have as a Warrior is this: **Boundaries are not mean. Boundaries are relief.**

I want to share a personal example of this freedom. I have a brother who has struggled his whole life. For years, I tried to help him. I tried to save him. I took on his chaos as my own. It drained me. It made me sick. Eventually, I had to shut the door. I had to set a boundary that said, *"I love you, but I cannot take care of you anymore."*

The moment I shut that door, I didn't feel guilty. **I felt relief**. I felt a physical weight lift off my chest. I realized that by refusing to participate in his dysfunction, I was actually freeing both of us. I was freeing myself from his negative energy, and I was freeing him to face his own life.

I have another example—an ex-boyfriend. He was an alcoholic. It was a difficult relationship. But years later, we are friends. Why? Because I have boundaries. I don't rely on him. I don't try to fix him. I maintain the friendship out of compassion because I know he is a good person struggling with a demon. Because my boundaries are titanium, I can offer him kindness without getting sucked back into his swamp.

This is the Warrior's power: **You can love people without losing yourself.** You can stand in a room full of crazy and remain sane, because you know exactly where you end and they begin.

Embracing the Shadow: Living Authentically

The Survivor hides their flaws because they are afraid of being attacked. The Warrior exposes their flaws because they know they cannot be used against them.

This is called **Living Authentically**. It means accepting the *whole* you. Not just the nice parts. Not just the "spiritual" parts. But the parts of you that have made mistakes. The parts of you that have been cruel.

I look back at my life, and I am not proud of everything I have done. There were times I was mean. There were times I was selfish. There were times I hurt people because I was hurting. I don't hide that. I don't pretend I am a saint. I look at those moments and say, *"Yes, I did that. That was a part of my journey. I learned from it, and I chose to be different."*

When you embrace your own darkness—your own capacity to be messy—you become bulletproof. Shame cannot survive in the light of ownership. If someone comes to you and says, *"You were a terrible friend ten years ago,"* the Warrior doesn't get defensive. The Warrior says, *"You are right. I was going through a lot, and I didn't have the tools I have now. I am sorry."*

That helps you accept yourself. The good and the bad. Because we are all a mix of both. When you stop fighting your own history, you have so much more energy to create your future.

The Weapon of Gratitude

How do we keep our vibration high? How do we stop slipping back into the depression of the Victim? We use the most powerful weapon in our arsenal: **Gratitude.**

Now, I don't mean a toxic positivity "everything is great" gratitude. I mean a strategic shift in focus. Your brain is a search engine. If you type in "Why is my life hard?" it will give you a million results. If you type in "What is working right now?" it will give you a million results.

I make it a daily habit to find the gratitude. It shifts your focus from what is going *wrong* to what is going *right.*

The Ripple Effect: Gratitude isn't just internal; it is relational. If I wake up and think, *"I am so grateful for my friend,"* that is a nice thought. But if I pick up my phone and text that friend, *"Hey, I was just thinking about how much you support me, and I appreciate you,"* now I have created a reality.

- I feel better.
- She feels better.
- The bond between us gets stronger.

That is Warrior magic. You are creating a positive feedback loop in your life. You are training the people around you to operate in love and appreciation, simply by embodying it yourself.

The Lesson of Uncertainty: The COVID Reality

Finally, we must address the ultimate enemy of the Warrior: **The Illusion of Control.**

If there is one thing we have all learned recently, it is that we are not in charge. Look at COVID. In the blink of an eye, the world shut down. Plans were cancelled. Jobs were lost. People died. Life as we knew it evaporated overnight.

It was terrifying. But it was also the greatest lesson in **Impermanence** we will ever receive. It taught us that the future is not promised. It taught us that our 5-year plans are just guesses. It taught us that the only thing we actually possess is **Today**.

The Victim looks at uncertainty and panics. *"What if it happens again? What if I lose everything?"* The Warrior looks at uncertainty and says, *"I cannot control the world. I can only control myself."*

Because we know that life can change in a snap, we stop waiting.

- We don't wait to forgive.
- We don't wait to say "I love you."
- We don't wait to wear the nice dress or use the good china.

We live *now*. We appreciate the roof over our heads *now*, because we know it isn't guaranteed. We appreciate our health *now* because we know how fragile it is.

This isn't morbid. It is vitalizing. It makes the colors of life brighter. When you realize that *this* moment is the only one you have, you stop wasting it on petty arguments or old resentments. You squeeze every drop of joy out of it.

The Final Charge

You are ready. You have the tools. You have the mindset. You have the heart.

You know that No Loss is just a loss. Every single thing that has happened to you—the abuse, the sickness, the heartbreak—was a lesson designed to bring you to this exact moment of power. You are not a survivor of your life; you are the Author of it.

Go out there. Set your boundaries. Speak your truth. Love yourself fiercely. And when the world tries to knock you down—and it will—remember who you are. You are a Warrior. And Warriors don't break. We just bounce back higher.

Actionable Step: The Daily Warrior Checklist

To finish this book, I want to give you a practical tool. This is your daily alignment check. Print this out. Put it on your fridge. Do not go to sleep until you have checked these boxes in your mind.

1. The Purpose Check:

- *Did I do one thing today that aligned with my values?*

(e.g., "I was patient with my kids," "I worked on my project," "I helped a stranger.")

2. The Boundary Check:

- *Did I say 'Yes' when I wanted to say 'No'?*

If yes, forgive yourself, and plan how to fix it tomorrow.

- *Did I protect my peace today?*

3. The Gratitude Check:

- *Identify 3 things that went **right** today.*

(e.g., "The coffee was hot," "The traffic was light," "I felt strong during my workout.")

- *Did I express that gratitude to anyone?*

4. The Authenticity Check:

- *Was I real today?*
- *Did I hide my feelings, or did I own them?*

5. The Release:

- Close your eyes. Visualize the stress of the day as a gray smoke.
- Breathe it out.
- Say: *"I release what I cannot control. I am enough."*

You have the map. You have the fuel. Now, drive.

EPILOGUE

This book has been an exploration of resilience, of turning trauma into strength, and of reshaping the narrative from victimhood to empowered survival. The path to becoming a **Conqueror** is not always easy, but it is one worth every step.

I have learned that every scar, every wound, is a chapter in the story that shapes us. These painful experiences have carved out spaces in my heart and soul that have led me to a greater sense of purpose. The truth I have come to understand is simple yet profound: Pain is not the enemy. It is the spark for transformation. Through the fire, we are molded into the strongest versions of ourselves.

For so long, I carried the weight of my past, believing it defined me. I held onto the labels of victimhood, fragility, and brokenness. But with each challenge, I released those labels bit by bit. And in doing so, I discovered a deeper truth: We are not defined by what happens to us, but by how we rise from it. The Warrior within each of us is always there, ready to rise. I know that God has guided me through the darkest moments, providing the strength I needed to overcome when I thought I had nothing left.

We are not defined by our wounds, but by our ability to heal, to grow, and to rise above them. We are the authors of our own stories, and the chapters that follow are ours to write.

This book is for those who have endured, for those who still find themselves in the trenches, for those who wonder if they'll ever find peace. You are not broken. You are not lost. You are never alone. The road may be difficult, but the strength you'll find along the way will be worth every step.

Thank you for walking this path with me. You are my inspiration.

About the Author

Deborah Ann Tome, LCSW, is a dedicated Licensed Clinical Social Worker with over four decades of experience in the mental health field. Throughout her career, Deborah has worked tirelessly to support individuals through various forms of trauma, providing therapy, counseling, and guidance across diverse populations. She is a seasoned practitioner, well-versed in therapeutic modalities such as Cognitive Behavioral Therapy (CBT), Dialectical Behavior Therapy (DBT), and Mindfulness-based approaches.

Deborah has spent years serving both in-home and office-based therapy clients, working with a wide range of issues, including trauma, addiction, and mental health challenges. Her experience spans from clinical work with the geriatric population to offering support for individuals with severe medical and mental health conditions. As the owner and operator of her private practice since 2011, Deborah has built a reputation for her compassionate and effective approach to mental health care.

In her prior roles, Deborah served as the Director at the University of Hawaii at Hilo, where she directed a highly successful drug prevention and treatment program. She wrote grants, developed programs, and created an interactive television show that linked island leaders in drug prevention and education. Her work gained national attention and recognition, with the program being named "Student Program of the Year" by the U.S. Department of Education. Deborah's leadership in these projects exemplifies her commitment to innovative solutions in the mental health field.

Deborah has also contributed to the mental health field through leadership roles in organizations such as Millwood Hospital and Dallas Metrocare, where she provided clinical supervision, developed programs, and advocated for improved service standards. Her dedication to quality management and regulatory compliance has earned her multiple accolades and recognition throughout her career.

Beyond her clinical work, Deborah has been an advocate for mental health through her leadership positions on various boards, including serving on the NASW Board of Directors for the State of Hawaii. She is a nationally recognized speaker, having spoken on a variety of psychological topics and presented at numerous professional conferences.

Deborah holds a Master's Degree in Social Work from Portland State University and has been continuously pursuing professional development through advanced coursework and certifications. With a rich and varied career, she brings both personal and professional experience to her work, empowering others to heal and thrive in the face of adversity.

www.ingramcontent.com/pod-product-compliance
Ingram Content Group UK Ltd.
Pitfield, Milton Keynes, MK11 3LW, UK
UKHW020124290926
15471UKWH00003B/260

9 798295 748257